MW01228329

JACK
or
In those Days, Jack Henry Claire was not that Rare

a poetry collection
by
e. smith sleigh

Poetry Books:

NINE LINES for Emily Dickinson
THESE THINGS Are A One Thing
OUR NATURE/THIS NATURE
MUSINGS FROM THE FAULT LINE AFTER DARK
AN AMERICAN STILL LIFE
VERITY IS RELATIVE: Emma's Memoir
CATCH A LOVER FALLING
CATCH A LOVER FALLING part II
For images, excerpts, blog, illustrations
and ordering information visit:
http://esmithsleigh.weebly.com/

Artistrie & Associates
revised edition 2020

*Poems Index placed at the end of the collection.

In this revised edition, **Jack Henry Claire** is the man you know or have heard of, the guy next door, your friend's cousin. Jack is the troublesome guy who gets away with everything, or nothing, and or meets his end. His exploits, his maneuvers, are means to obtain what he desires. The women he encounters are the narrators of Jack's adventures and the devastation Jack causes.

dust storms

he tried to catch a cloud
then he attempted to seize dust blowing
across desert terrain
he tried to possess me

he never understood impossibilities

he liked secret alcoves in dark dusty club alleys,

he ignored crashes on misty mountain roads

and he didn't comprehend that heart attacks might
occur after contentious business meetings

-- e. smith sleigh

something solar

who obliterated the crown of the sun
the only forgiveness they'll obtain from the gods
will be their climb up Olympus or into the Rockies
where they will view the sun backwards
and mend it with a mirror or a hologram

  did you ever meet someone who is always hungry
    for a ménage   a martini   mincemeat

he took a hundred years to grow older
standing in the dusty fallow field
he looked at the burning, open door
and entered it singing 'we all shine on'

-- e. smith sleigh

I'll never call you

blue and white were the colors of the room
after midnight it all faded to a swirling black
I'm leaving occurred to me
while I watched you sleep

covalent relationships
it's me whispering in your ear
"I won't call you later tonight,
tomorrow or ever"

clothed in shadows
your nude body asleep
begs for   touching
but I don't

I'm always leaving
gotta go, before you follow

to be human,
is not divine

  four days of snow came down

-- e. smith sleigh

previously published in RAR (Rat's Ass Review)

triangulate

it's the desert for the promising
silent vastness has no signifier for denied
possibilities

as he walked by   he shouted
'impossible about the possibilities'

now too late the impossible-possibilities arrive wearing
snow gear
or is it desert gear
he's culpable   non linear
no movement   trapezoidal head's unclear
no doubt   pack the Lincoln   sign out

-- e. smith sleigh

seeker

on the lake, a pale moonlight
floats below the roofline, the moon hovers
silhouettes the house

the stars are gone

inside, love is hidden
and lies in his hands
cupped like a shelter
built for enduring things

but she was gone
he cradled his hands against his heart

belying his credence
of loving lightly, slightly
like a small, fretful bird

-- e. smith sleigh

jewelry

a trick of the mind   a long running theme of a dip in the
warm currents   and the cold waters of time

I want to say I couldn't love you more   but there is more

clap your hands   swim channels to reach an end   not
this end   not this place on the other side of the universe
or this island seashore   charming fixations dwell here
you can consume them and not gain shame

yes I would love you more   I could have loved you less,
I loved you just enough but your other lovers sapped my
love

dance with me now   in the waters off the island
just after the sun's rise   understand   I cannot make
this permanent   do you recognize your lies on my lips
and in my eyes

I feel drops of water running down my chest   dripping
off my breasts   we have this time together   there is
swirling turquoise around us   Jack, I can't give you
more than that

-- e. smith sleigh

on Aegina

   pistachio's bitter woody seed coat
the tan shell lining left on the
nuts grown on one of the Greek isles
is bitter and pungent

   he tasted the paper-like
fragment in the back of his throat
brought it forth and spat it on the ground

   no ancient presence in the Aegean
can remove that lingering tang on the tip of his tongue
like the taste of Greek girls whose genitals always
smelled of the sea or olive oil
or the boys who liked the coins mixed with
the pistachios he carried in his pocket

   his choice of companions was always carelessly made
his adventures in the islands occasionally ended with the
gnashing of teeth, someone crying, and money
exchanged

   he introduced the two padres, universalist and
orthodox although from divergent worlds they were
infatuated with one another   too much denial made
them eager

   he enjoyed watching them in their
slow dance to hell   if they ever found it
   myths die hard and hide many things

he walked by the blazing charcoal bricks
where the nuts were roasted   he relished the
taste of those wonderful meats   he also liked the
smell of the heat

let's see   who else did he introduce
oh yes there was this guy named something like
brick, rock, or stone to a spectacular Brazilian
transvestite

and those women, several traveling lesbians who
passed as bored hetero wives   he enjoyed being a
matchmaker for them   he gave the gift of Sapphic love
to all the wives

in his life he only loved two people, a couple from his
college days   a twosome recruited for a threesome
they chose not to travel with him to the isles   he longed
for them -- scrumptious feasts

he always took pleasure in taunting humanity with its
baubles and babbles   and sexual foibles
he waited   hungry   like an expectant spider
somehow time slows when you're told you're dying

he thought why pay attention to the Abramic religions
that always seemed to be roasting someone pistachio-
like   heating skins and nuts extracted for the
deliciousness of some sin   or ritual

he understood all cocoons and sweetmeats have bitter
coverings

-- e. smith sleigh

predictable in retrospect

   stormy crosswinds near the cliff
he challenges spectators
to guess his identity
just as a Gallic cross appears
near the Spin Ghar mountains
Khyber pass
perpendicularity

   fiddler asks who profits
from the games of Armageddon and
words doused with petrol
mediums doused with psychosis
and earth doused
with his no-regrets

-- e. smith sleigh

a grey market

popular grey color manufactured by a man
on a rainy day

the grey haired men who color their hair
who barely retain their footing
on slate grey rocky ground

the fading patriarchs
slide into the stony grey morass of a
self-created disintegration   grey-blue dusk

nocturnal   disk diffidence
slick moss-covered dark grey stone
a fording of the symbolic stream

parallel silver portals decorated with
striations of achromatic grey color schemes

the blend of lead metal tints   lost
grey smoke from a grey haystack
streaks the grey monochromatic sky

egregious, grey, rapier eyes
leave in the darkest, steel grey limousines

-- e. smith sleigh

outing

   near her house, at daybreak, as time stretches away
from the night's heat   trees sway

   pushed by the sunrise breezes   they samba
together they turn into a green yellow-brown shadow

birds sing tin-roof chants to the backyard emptiness
they perch on swinging limbs and ride a tilt-a-whirl
the red rose bush bows to greet the morning again
                            and again

strange tropical tree flecks its pods at anxious,
   barking dogs that warn of the skulking neighbor who
sculpts the metal fence into a concave bow,
   it's a monument to his obsession with
                     what he cannot possess

-- e. smith sleigh

always exonerated

sunlight drops
through
dew drops

life   like honey
blunders forgiven for a repair
 or a song

-- e. smith sleigh

graph

    on occasion she divides into two   back bent she
labors   her intensity is the rapture of visions   the
dynamic solitude of dreams

    she is a raptor spewing forth words and declarations of
experience and lessons learned , love and loss -- grief
for the earth she adores and soon will leave

    another part of her denies the truth she seeks   she no
longer toils at the desk bathed in candles' light   some
days she reclines into misgivings

    she tries to understand it all   but her natural rhythms
were pilfered by her struggle with the male-organized
pretense in life

    rivulets run down the glass   slow   icy   the texture of
Van Gogh's paintings comes to her mind

-- e. smith sleigh

some play in winter

she lay there in the tub   still
  like the stacked white towels by the sinks:

afterward I stared into the dark
studying the cityscape and the sky

I wanted to   cry   scream
it was so   rough

come dawn   he was gone the streaks in the bathroom
marble turned into Tibetan dancing figures   and one
face

the suite was cold and the snow began to fall
slow-like   straight down to the hellscape below

I prayed   I begged   please send me something crazy
I mean really crazy good crazy

  I want affirmation   prove to me I'm still alive
  that this was   somehow   necessary

-- e. smith sleigh

look

leave my heart alone
for it is not my heart you seek
you seek my body
  to spend like money

and then retreat   back
behind your bedroom door
  non-siren-like but bellowing

you selected the coinage
from your bag of memories
you're mad at something
  or someone you
  want more or less from

you are a hunter of bodies
a seeker of unenduring love
  but your old habits are boring

  you closed your eyes, your heart
  and marched through the door
  into some fantasy, onto another fuck
    or to your grave

-- e. smith sleigh

portents

naturally, she walked in an extra self-conscious way
when he came to town   just for moments he would turn
aside his private fantasies

he remained awake through regrets and pain produced
by his obligatory attachment to his familial nightmare
this accounted for much of his over-the-top, off-a-bit
joviality

and the savagery of the attempted rape
applied cruelty exacted in a quite alien way to her

she was a gift presented to him by her parents
she was their giveaway to a man who preferred
other activities than female attention

after they were married
her parents sent her back when she tried to run

-- e. smith sleigh

irony

a decade is burning on the floor in front of you
slide your card down and help the situation

hold your phone until it scars your hand
put the cell to your head until you stroke out
slay the 'lectric blue beast
stomp the paper label on the tin can

how was the word *change* poisoned
do say the word stop

the fiend in him watches
gazing
into the sky
poised to graze on you

a moment ago she passed the just go sign
someone whom she hates   holds her hand

-- e. smith sleigh

interloper

the 'lectric blue is silenced now
smart schedules and lineups once followed her around

she pleaded for someone to stop the yelling
creaming screaming porn   finally, she broke the TV

any-act-freaky-box blocked-blood-red-head
dead on arrival   but not really   she later recovered

he ran out of his little blue pills
his un-drugged silence followed her around

she pursued the stillness down to the shore
into the white and turquoise sea

-- e. smith sleigh

window world

I saw the man who lives in the house across the street
skitter by the open blinds like a waterbug   seconds
became minutes

inanity movements become menacing in full light
dancing ensued inside the house

he has a wife and too little girls that he frightens but he
likes to start with beating the dogs

"the neighbors only drive you crazy
because you let them"

but the man, what about the man   something inside him
"needs fixing"

-- e. smith sleigh

d'oro thy   don

one day I will run into you   I will not recognize you
and you will know it   you   jaded dated overrated
over the rainbow   scarecrow   follow the yellow brick
road   did you say you're not in Kansas anymore

old   old post card from Leavenworth or was it OZ
and points north   is it funny   no one laughs anymore
talk to me now   did you have all the fun no one
expected you to

you abused   do you whisper it to yourself   on those
rare occasions   when you acknowledge the darkest
shadow that moves across the mirror   officer and a what
but you're a clean machine   right

I told you   "your daughter's dead"

you said   "that's too bad"

-- e. smith sleigh

mythology bites from Milton Banana

dead lies live   Rasputin lies   attempted tricks of the
mind all 222 boyfriend/husband myths to make you
forget what you know to be true   or see   or
remember

15 it's not what it seems   26 I don't know honey
38 I didn't do it   41 they didn't mean anything to me
45 that's your imagination   59 I don't know,
she/he was just there   beams in on the quiet moments
demolishing   producing anguish and pain   120
deceptions from the male who wants to reign in his
hogan of lies and half truths   excuses and myths always
lead back to his service in Pinal County 85222

-- e. smith sleigh

published in PANKHEARST: Slimline Volume NO LOVE
LOST "Mythology Bites from Chilton Banana" p. 7

reptile ways

it's not that what you're saying doesn't make sense,
it doesn't

do you know what I'm saying   it's that I can't   I won't
I will not accommodate you on your bad days   in your
horny hours   looking   for something-strange days

I won't change my voice   my hair   my clothes   my
way of walking   talking   to become the object of
your photo-infatuation-stimulation in the bathroom   or
garage   or drive home   no it's not that I won't   it's
that I have the will not to

it's that you don't understand betrayal   but I will betray
you because you betray in the most ridiculous ways
it's not that you sometimes act like a creep   it's that I
don't want to be seen with a creep

no   I can't really

it's that I no longer care about what you play with
sacrifice or fuck   fuck your goats   can't you clean
that inbred act up, just a bit   not that I wouldn't go for
your excuses I did   it's that   not now   I refuse to
pimp the world to you

I won't lead anything with an orifice to you and look the
other way   are you in pain   is the pain shooting
through your arm again

it's not what you're thinking   you will have surgery on
that shoulder   elbow   wrist   when you're older   your
hand can tell you the reasons for your carpal tunnel
you know, anything in excess

don't try to deny your preferences
no myth excuses them
take a big drink of absinthe
and don't forget to swallow

then crawl to your no-home
the one you created with your lies

-- e. smith sleigh

freedom is just a moment away

I trip over the knitting basket where just a few seconds
ago kittens played   they cherish the life   swim in the air
are enthralled by the dance   a mid flight samba

I hear a door creak   he threatens to take them away   but
slips and falls on the kitchen floor

once I saw a cat dance down a road on his way
to the end of it

-- e. smith sleigh

distorted

a forged peace floats through on occasion   giving me a
false sense of security   providing me with an excuse to
plan for normal hours   normal activities

I remind myself the feeling is counterfeit   the moments
are fake   I am weak   I deny   I deny

 to deny   is not autonomy   yet I give myself a few
minutes of life as it was   I feel the years of my freedom
in a world and with a man yet to go mad   but teetering

--e. smith sleigh

tab

shallow is a man's mind when it comes to
women   a male finds it difficult to
believe any woman could ever become bored with him
his schedules   his routine   his same ol' things
his same ol' words   same ol' moves   same ol' sex

no hint works   no change is made

then she leaves for always

and for ever

he wonders why

-- e. smith sleigh

NONE

ONE FIREFLY IN THE RAIN
TWO DOE IN THE ROAD
TWO RAVEN IN THE TALL TREES
THREE CATS IN THE WINDOW SILL
STILL

FOUR EARLY BERRIES ON THE HOLLY
FIVE GOLDENRODS BY THE DRIVE
ONE LAKE BELOW ME
ONE OLD MAN INSIDE THE HOUSE
BARELY ALIVE
NOT BY ME
OR BY MY HAND
OR IN MY MIND
BUT BY HIS HAND

ONE YOUNG WOMAN ON THE SIDEWALK
ALONE
OR GONE

-- e. smith sleigh

declaration

I watched his eyes skate up and down my crossed legs
he became distracted and after a minute or two
he stopped talking altogether

I was pleased that he noticed
but I was surprised and a little annoyed at his weakness
that he claimed he didn't possess

but seemed to possess him
question was how many other legs
stopped him so easily

my answer was
of course, he did this many times
and will do it again

I don't know
he declared himself bisexual a while ago

-- e. smith sleigh

into the game

many powers have been attributed to the moon
concerted mission tales ending

maltreated boys crying for their toys
       'they gonna play beneath the bridge
       don't follow them'

they say he was here before the moon and me

now and again I think about
the way things used to be

eight days into the game

-- e. smith sleigh

asphalt conveyance II

you will never drive my car
or burn anything in the back seat
are you wondering
or is your mind wandering

because you will have to find
another way out
no games and no quarter

the sexy commercial luxury-
capitalist-cum-communist mirage is death in this
suburban good-life-porch-bmw-mercedes-
carbon-monoxide-choked pavement
beaming heat waves back at the sun

dark blue-black cars driven slowly on the road
time rises fast on a sinister concrete sea of
shake and show and go away

-- e. smith sleigh

a specter in manland

I lived during the tattering
    during the take down

I lived during the exploitative use
of a devolved language of manipulation

they severed heads
the mislead were redirected into worship houses
chained to stop signs or hung from bridges

I lived during the conduit crash
    during the denied dollar crash
    during the times of economic slaughter
     falsified misdirection   denied   takings
     contracts placed on those who looked under
      covers and in files and dared to show or tell

l lived during the punishments for existing
I lived during the glorification of self-appointed male
deities that stand by while other humans suffer and die
there were declarations about the threats of child-eating
demons

I lived during the era of massacres caused by
   misguided thoughts and fantasies

we lived during the carnage
        during the no-win no-lose
          corporations for-prophet-wars
        during the playing at a society
        during the acts of kindnesses that weren't

theft from children   theft of children
deaths after the abuse of children
permission given to any male and his belief system
        to maraud
        to persecute
        desiccate
        rape of body or mind

-- e. smith sleigh

son of acid

you were the product of poisons
the son of acids you sallied forth
to do your parents deeds for them
always under their control

you carried your acrid payload
in the vial that was your body
spewed it in strange smells
at inappropriate times it filled the night air
frequently kept your prey,
the woman, at bay

you grew to be their nightmare,
their Hamburg scary movie
disgorging things from your mouth
you assaulted like a raptor

you operate on feigned innocence
silence   predator instinct
you cajoled   ravaged   rampaged
you claimed to be the victim
you handled snakes and extracted their venom
and spread it like butter

does your mouth still smell,
like the cankered bowels of slain gods

-- e. smith sleigh

to abandon a dream

I resist

when you defy   when you try   to stand on your own
when you don't have and you strive to have   at some
point when they comprehend you can outwit them   the
scheming   the whining begins
the cajole   major con of some kind   the alibi
the structured lie

I resist

if you ignore them   they threaten   there's manipulation
the blowup   the blow   they will step in front of you and
try to stop your forward momentum

at that moment you are really on your own   they use the
ultimate punishment   threatened abandonment   if
they can't force you to abandon a dream   they will
abandon you

I resist

in my mind   a few years ago
I discarded all of them

-- e. smith sleigh

abide

I lived with you when
I couldn't

I lived without you
when I thought I couldn't
live with you

I loved someone else
when I thought I couldn't
love again
I still want to…

no confession here
but you know
and you know why

I live without you
when I thought I wouldn't

-- e. smith sleigh

javelin

   he's a no fade, no fake paradigm
archetype   fantasy gourmand
creator of torn discourse and days

   his actions make me repeat stultifying things
over and over again in my mind
   hateful counterpoints don't take over for long
because I project

   waterways   surrounding creeks hiking paths
   and wind upon the sails

I remember how nettles in the fence rows
are health hazards
my situation occurs to me

   endangered from bouts of vileness
   finding desolation in change
   an always cruel, old man Dismay
   uses such a worn out cliché, but the cliché still hurts
   non-proven point replicating on eardrums produces
   time donuted into a severity of living days

holding his hand or patting his back
gives no comfort to him

-- e. smith sleigh

conservator

there's a rhythm to hurt like this
　and it's not breaking waves

does his ghost precede him
the white sands move ever eastward

wait for the desiccation　judge his actions as he judges
you　　as he pushes you toward the nucleus of his
demands

no one who survived the death of a daughter or a
relationship should be sent to this verdict, this harsh
something in nothing

continued injuries from human ignorance
his arrogance　this heated hormone parchedness creeps
across earthscapes

I'll consider the ecology of the landscape not the
desiccation

not his pleasure or his gratification

-- e. smith sleigh

21st century knight

  what challenge did you think you issued
what gauntlet did you believe you threw to the ground
when you turned love into a jigsaw puzzle
when you made love a riddled word
when you dipped your pen into the font
of tumbled-down
upside down no love

  ok you killed love at your leisure
as a true sportsman
a hunter of the hearts of women, and men
a member in the club
of wrathful love

  a remote   pornography   a pill
are all you need   these actions are a
self-designed armageddon

you lost the world's respect and mine
your horse   your sword   your armor
your medals   your metal   long ago

-- e. smith sleigh

thrash about

I thought I saw you in the moonlight shadows
beyond the columns were you beckoning me
into the dark I'll never know because I will never follow
you

a cold   lonesome chill passes over me
  do you understand I will never follow

I will be lost   separate

    still

I will never

follow you again

-- e. smith sleigh

breathe

block wall makes me hyperventilate
closed in   close   too close

glass bricks look like an opaque non-world
like the world of an infant
fighting to see
   fighting to hear
     confused at the
              confusing

red brick the color of the womb
                    translucent

yes I remember

I wonder
                at what might have been

-- e. smith sleigh

spring waters

   will you wander the terrain
with something other than your feet

wade the ocean shorelines in a mind trance

   when you walk in the eddying tidal basins
use a carefully curated jovial manner
a bolstered stride

   perhaps a dance on tiptoes will do well there
where the crabs and water snakes dwell

  beware the dying man who charges a fee
to predict the end of anything or everything
remember our sentient earth

   walk lightly in the waters of spring,
the early waters

    that chill

-- e. smith sleigh

some syndrome

you sit there and cry again
you took a seat and still you reach
for what you can no longer touch
you cannot help yourself

I wish you did not feel the hurt of your days
I feel your uneasiness I believe the anguish you suffer

do you recognize the wounds you inflicted on me
I hope no one else will undergo your sting

does it make you feel better when I'm not in the room

death sits beside you   sometimes I see you look at him
you recognize he's going to take you

I don't want you to go   you are all that I know
with or without your pain   or mine

-- e. smith sleigh

nowhere to be found

I'll throw poetry in the water
and bellow 'I remember'
still
I'm losing time
and skylines …
and, of course, Jack Henry Claire
who was never really there
or mine

-- e. smith sleigh

wills

the song that I am listening to
has the man I never met in it

somewhere within
this soothing melody
the words question love although
they produce a calm near the end

where is that steady man
where is that tender and tough man
where is the balance

--e. smith sleigh

Poem Index

Poem Title

dust storms
something solar
I'll never call you
triangulate
seeker
jewelry
on Aegina
predictable in retrospect
a grey market
outing
always exonerated
graph
some play in winter
look
portents
irony
interloper
window world
d'oro thy don
mythology bites from Chilton Banana
reptile ways
freedom is just a moment away
distorted
tab
NONE

Poem Title

declaration
into the game
asphalt conveyance II
a specter in manland
son of acid
to abandon a dream
abide
javelin
conservator
21st century knight
thrash about
breathe
spring waters
some syndrome
nowhere to be found
wills

BIO

e. smith sleigh writes poetry and fiction, won awards for her writing and lives by a lake in Robert Penn Warren country where she draws inspiration. She is a pioneer in discussions, tweets, and blogs about post structuralism on the internet. She blogs about post-structuralism and literature on her website http://esmithsleigh.weebly.com/

Sleigh's first poetry book is entitled These Things are a One Thing. Her following books are: Our Nature/This Nature, Musings from the Fault Line after Dark and An American Still Life. sleigh's newest poetry book is Catch a Lover Falling. Her non-fiction book is entitled: Post Structuralism and Related Quotes: from Jacques Derrida, Judith Kristeva, and Many Others. Her fiction book is Sibbe's Way, an historical fiction account of northern European ancestry. sleigh's Verity is Relative: Emma's Memoir was written in prose and poetry as a fictional memoir.

She was nominated for her state's 2013-2014 Poet Laureate. Her 5th poetry book, <u>An American Still Life</u>, appeared on the list for the 2016 Pulitzer Poetry Prize.

Made in the USA
Columbia, SC
02 September 2020